The Kweendom™ Presents:

Drama Queen to Peace Kween

Seven Gems To Peacefully Handle
Disputes In Your Kweendom™

Kween Mingo

Table of Contents

Copyright

Dedication

For the four quadrants of my heart: Kianna, Timia, TJ, and Kameron. I love you more than the air in my lungs.

The Kweendom™ Presents:

Drama Queen to Peace Kween

Introduction

Have you ever had a full-on disagreement with a friend or family member and felt like you were talking to a wall? Have you ever tried explaining yourself only to realize the other person isn't truly listening?

Listening is a skill that few people possess. So when you're blessed with this skill, it's your duty to be a blessing to others.

And my listening skills have helped countless people do just that.

I am a Libra... a stone-cold Libra at my core (shoutout to all my Libras!!!). I seek balance and fairness in all aspects of my life. So it's no surprise that I am the go-to person for everyone in my circle. My friends, parents, siblings... you name it. They all come to me to balance their issues. And I absolutely love it!

As a child, I used to sit in my mother's kitchen and listen intently to her conversations with her friends (I know, I know: I was NOT staying in a "child's place"). I could only hear one side of the conversation but it wasn't hard to figure out what was going on. After listening to my mother complain about her friend complaining, I remember asking her to just help her friend find a solution so she doesn't have to hear her friend complain. At the time, I didn't realize I was acting partially as a mediator. I didn't even know there was such a thing as a mediator, but I knew I loved the feeling of helping my mother's friend find the solution to her problem.

The reality is, most people put their own interests, needs, and feelings first. Most people allow egos, emotions, and pride to inhibit their ability to think logically. And if you can filter through all the muck in the emotions, real solutions can be found.

As a mediator and arbitrator, I am able to filter through the junk that hinders people from finding real solutions.

The purpose of this brief manual, is to help anyone who struggles with conflict of any kind, find ways to come up with solutions to your problems. This book will help all the *Drama Queens become Peace Kweens* while sitting pretty in their Kweendom™.

Chapter 1
Clarify the Disagreement

Let's keep it ALL THE WAY 100!!! How many times have you been in an argument and then you realize that you don't even know what the argument is *TRULY* about? Come on now, we have all had that moment when we are trying to tell the story of an argument to one of the homies and you say something like, "I don't even know how it got started". It's happened to us all.

When attempting to find a happy medium (a solution that all parties agree on), the first step is to *clarify what the disagreement really is* at that point. This seems like a simple principle but it carries a lot of weight. Just think for a second, how can you truly get to the bottom of a disagreement if you're not even on the same page as the other party, regarding what the disagreement is all about?

As a mediator, I can tell you there are countless times that I've encountered two parties who are in dispute but they aren't on the same page regarding what the dispute is about. You may be wondering how this can be possible, but it is relatively easy to have two completely different stances on what the issue is at hand. For example, one person may think the argument is because the other party won't take him/her out for date nights, while the opposing party doesn't care about the dates. Instead, the issue for this party is the lack of quality time, that could include just sitting on the couch having an intimate conversation.

Another issue that many people run into is they don't agree on the severity of the disagreement. This happens a lot in marriages and long term relationships. It is not uncommon for one party to be at wits end and completely fed up with the issue while the other party has no clue that the problem is so severe that they are on the brink of separation.

So, how do you avoid being a Drama Queen and sit pretty in your Kweendom™ while becoming a Peace Kween? How do you make sure all parties are aware of the severity of the disagreement? You simply ask for clarity.

Peace Kween Tips on Gaining Clarity

1. Admit you need clarity when you truly don't understand. Don't allow pride or ego to get in the way of you getting a better understanding of the disagreement. Simply stating, "I don't understand", can open the dialogue for a better understanding of the issue.

2. Refrain from gaslighting. Gaslighting is a form of emotional abuse that causes the other person to question their own reality. By gaslighting, the gaslighter isn't attempting to gain clarity on the disagreement. Instead, they are attempting to undermine the other party's perception of reality. And we all know it will be pretty difficult to come to a resolution if you're not living in reality.

3. Be specific. Sometimes you just don't want to hurt the other person's feelings. And you may think you're doing yourself a favor, but you definitely are not. Be specific with your grievances. This isn't

to be confused with being harsh or rude. You can be specific and honest without being rude. Plus, remember Drama Queens are rude. Peace Kweens attempt to have peace in their hearts, before giving someone else a piece of their mind.

4. Ask open-ended questions. For example, instead of saying, "did you always feel this way about me", try "when did you first notice you were feeling this way". Asking open-ended questions allows the conversation to flow better, providing better clarity.

5. Discuss your issues over food. When I do mediations, I almost always have some type of food available. Usually, it isn't a full meal but I will definitely have snacks. Why? Because people tend to be more open and forthcoming with their thoughts when they are nibbling on food. This small gesture has helped resolve many conflicts.

Chapter 2
Figure Out the Common Goal

Now that you and the other person are on the same page and have an understanding of what the disagreement is and the degree of severity, now you need to get clarity on the common goal.

This is a step in the peaceful resolution process that is often overlooked but it is so critical. Having an understanding of the common goal can help you and the other party reach the resolution faster. It will also allow you to strategically work together to achieve the goal.

For example, let's imagine you are in Mediation to Stay Married to your spouse (yes, Kween, mediation to stay married is a REAL thing and is completely different than marriage counseling - but we will save that for another book). You and your significant other are both in agreement that the issue at hand is that you both are feeling slightly bored in your marriage. That magical, butterflies in your stomach feeling have melted away. Your activities have become very predictable and there is no longer any excitement. So where do you go from here? You figure out the common goal.

While discussing this with the other party, you may learn that you have two completely different goals. One person may want to enjoy having sex more often, while the other party may want to change their typical routine and add excitement. The only way to know for sure is to talk about what the goal is and work towards it. So, how do you figure out the common goal? Flip the script for a few tips to get to the bottom of your common goals.

Tips on Finding the Common Goal

1. Set clear expectations. Now isn't the time to be bashful or try to make the other party become a mind reader. The objective is to successfully reach your goals and you cannot do so if you aren't honest.

2. Ask. Yes, that's right. Ask the other party what their ultimate goal is and what they would like the outcome to be. This tip is so simple but is often one of the most missed components in dispute resolution.

3. Once you know what the common goal is, stay focused on the goal. Don't get sidetracked. Work every day towards your common goal.

4. Track your progress. Sometimes you may have to have meetings to discuss progress with the other party. You may benefit from writing down your goals and then tracking your progress in a journal.

5. Make an action plan. You've discovered your common goal but how are you going to reach your goal? Creating an action plan will outline the steps necessary to successfully reach your goal and it will also help you be able to visually see the wonderful progress you've made!

Chapter 3
Listen

It's pretty safe to say we all want to be understood. But how can you truly understand the other party's grievances if you don't actively LISTEN?

Listening connects each of us to another party and it is such a critical skill in life and in the art of dispute resolution. Often times, we think we are listening because we hear what the other party is saying but we are only listening to respond. We aren't taking in the other party's words.

Many people automatically assume actively listening benefits the person talking more than the person who is listening, because after all, the person expressing their grievances are being heard. But actively listening gives the listener an enormous amount of power.

By actively listening, you will improve your influence in resolving the dispute that can lead to persuading the other party during negotiations. Now, this tactic shouldn't be used for manipulation. That is not what I am saying here. What I am saying is by actively listening, you improve your power by gaining an understanding of the other person, thus allowing you to better negotiate your own grievances and goals. This is a win for everyone involved.

There are three specific listening structures most common in interpersonal communication; informational listening, critical listening, and therapeutic listening.

Informational Listening

Informational listening is simply listening to learn. This is one of the most utilized forms of listening. Informational listening happens every day. We participate in informational listening when we watch the news, listen to a friend tell a story about their day, and listen to the weather report.

While it does take effort and concentration, informational listening is less active than the other two listening structures. With informational listening, we are literally listening to gain information. We aren't doing a lot of analyzing and/or criticizing in this structure, Kween.

Critical Listening

Critical listening is more active than informational listening. Critical listening is listening to analyze and evaluate. During critical listening, you are listening to scrutinize what is being said. This form of listening usually requires a decision to be made and/or problem to be solved. Similarly to critical reading, critical listening requires you to analyze the information provided in order to make an educated guess.

Therapeutic Listening

Therapeutic listening is basically putting yourself into the other party's shoes and attempting to understand the other party's feelings and emotions. This requires empathy, connecting with another person emotionally.

Therapeutic listening does not require you to offer any advice or make a deep analysis. Instead, you are encouraging the other party to elaborate on their feelings and emotions.

One of the main reasons why people don't actively listen is because they are impatiently waiting for their turn to talk. This comes off as selfish. You have to be willing to set aside your own agendas at that point and focus on the other party as they express themselves.

Active listening is truly a skill that can be learned over time. It requires much effort and restraint to keep yourself from interrupting the other party as they speak, especially when something that is said triggers your memory or makes what you feel is a valid counterargument. Waiting for your turn to speak is not an easy feat. So how do you overcome the need to jump in to speak while the other party is speaking? You're one flip away from tips on active listening.

Tips for Active Listening

1. Repeat what the person is saying in your head. This helps you retain the information being said and will help you recall the information later.

2. Repeat what was said back to the other party. Of course, you don't want to say every single detail verbatim as if you're some sort of artificially intelligent robot. But you do want to be able to recall pertinent details.

3. Do not interrupt. I know, I know. This is a hard one, especially if you disagree with what the other person is saying. But just know you will get a chance to speak. Plus, at this point, you all have already clarified what the disagreement is and what your common goal is so naturally, the next step is to listen intently without interruption. You've already made considerable progress and will continue to do so as you actively listen.

4. Listen to understand the other party's feelings and point of view. Remember you're not listening with the intentions to respond. Although you will have the opportunity to respond, this is the time that you should focus on what the other party is saying and feeling.

Chapter 4
Focus on the Solution

So at this point in the game, you are crystal clear on what the disagreement is all about. You also have figured out what your common goal is and you both have actively listened to one another. So, what's next?

Now, it's time to focus on the solution.

Too often, we focus on the problems and issues at hand. But at some point you have to move forward and focus on the solutions.

One of the first things you can do with the other party is figure out what you believe will work well. You can be as creative as you please. I encourage people in my sessions to think with your own parameters and not what you believe society says you should or should not do. This is your world and you can be as creative as you and the other party agree to be.

While creating and focusing on your solutions, start with a solution-based approach instead of problem-based questions. For example, a problem-based approach would be:

I wish I could buy that new car but I can't because I don't make enough money.

In contrast, a solution-focused approach would be:

What can I do to earn enough money to buy this new car?

Here's another example:

This isn't fair! How the hell did she get that promotion over me?

Solution Focused:

Let me put on my thinking cap and come up with some questions to ask her about how she was able to get promoted.

Essentially, focusing on the problems, makes you lose your power to solve the issue. By focusing on the solution, you have given yourself the authority to create steps to solving your problem.

Here are some traits of problem-focused individuals (aka Drama Queens):

1. They usually have a "whoa it's me" mentality. They typically feel hopeless and often won't accept responsibility for their own actions.

2. They give up easily. This is most often because of number 1. They feel they are so hopeless so there isn't a need to even try to move forward.

3. They often blame others for issues and shortcomings. Again, problem-focused individuals often have an issue with accepting responsibility for their own actions.

Here are some traits of solution-focused individuals (aka Peace Kweens):

1. They view problems as a challenge and are eager to find solutions. Solution-focused individuals realize there are solutions to every problem.

They know they can overcome problems and they actively seek out solutions instead of dwelling on the actual problem.

2. They take responsibility for their actions. Even when there is one major issue at hand, there is usually something that someone could have done differently to help contribute to a more favorable outcome.

3. They don't give up at the first sight of a problem. Solution-focused individuals will remain steadfast and push through the problem until they find a solution.

Tips for Focusing on Solutions and becoming a Peace Kween

1. Focus on your strengths. Once you have recognized what your strengths are, you are able to identify how to apply those strengths to solve the issues at hand.

2. Get clear on everyone's interests. While you may all have a common goal, your interests could be different. For example, you both may want to go to the local grocery store (common goal), but you may want to get sodas for dinner, while your partner may need to get cashback for the basketball game later today (different interest).

3. Focus on what each person can do. Refrain from focusing on what each person cannot do.

4. Discuss the options. We have already established that some

people easily give up when a problem presents. But you will be surprised how many possibilities there are to most problems.

Chapter 5
No Personal Attacks

1. You're so stupid.
2. Why can't you stop being so insecure?
3. You always want to argue.
4. Stop being so sensitive.
5. You never do anything right.
6. You always do that!
7. It's no wonder this marriage isn't working! You're an idiot.

While working towards solutions to your disputes, it is a great idea to refrain from personal attacks. I know, I know, you're probably thinking "DUH"! But in the heat of the moment, it is not uncommon to say hurtful things to the other party, but it is a bad idea.

Personal attacks can immediately put the other party on defense. Feeling attacked, makes the person attacked want to defend him/herself, and he/she may even want to retaliate. It could potentially become an ongoing cycle with no resolution in sight.

A personal attack also puts the attacker in the position of judgment, making the attacked person feel guilty. In the world of dispute resolution, there should be no judgments. No matter who one believes is right or wrong, all parties have a common goal and should be actively working towards that goal. By unleashing personal attacks, you run the risk of regressing during the dispute resolution process. This won't be good for anyone.

I understand we are all human, and sometimes, you just want to say the first thing that pops up in your mind but I urge you to think about your words before unleashing attacks.

Flip the script for tips to help you refrain from using personal attacks.

Tips to Help You Refrain From Using Personal Attacks

1. Take a deep breath. When you take a deep breath, it gives you a few extra seconds to think about what you want to say before you say it.

2. Reflect. While taking your deep breath, take a moment to reflect on what was said to you and how you want to respond. This will help you from instinctively saying the first thing that comes to your mind. This will give you the opportunity to choose your words wisely.

3. Don't immediately react. Again, taking that deep breath will give you just enough time to not immediately react to what was just said. Take a moment to ponder what was just said.

4. Don't retaliate. If the other party says something that is offensive, it is ok to let them know you are offended. However, you do not have to offend the other party in retaliation. I know, I know, our

mamas always told us, "if someone hits you, then hit them back... and harder" but retaliation won't get you very far and may even make the progress you have made go backward.

Chapter 6
Stick to One Dispute at a Time

Have you ever been having a heated discussion with someone and in the middle of trying to resolve one conflict, the other party brings up another issue, that is completely unrelated? Yes, I know you have because we all have.

Bringing up more issues before resolving the initial issue - or at least coming to an agreement to place the initial issue on pause for a while - only adds fuel to an already raging fire. And by doing so, you significantly reduce the chances of you resolving your disagreements.

Let me try to put things into perspective:

Imagine you and your significant other are having a pretty intense discussion about the toilet seat. You're upset because he never puts down the toilet seat. Last night, you woke up to go use the bathroom and fell into the toilet. You're pissed (no pun intended) and you want him to just put down the toilet seat.

While attempting to explain your point of view and why you shouldn't be subjected to such an atrocity, he states, "I just don't understand why you don't see the toilet seat is up and just put it down before you sit down! It's not that difficult, Brenda".

You reply, "I didn't want to wake you because I knew you had to get up and go to work at 4:30 this morning. I was being considerate, unlike you! You're never considerate of me and my needs. Just like that time we were at my sister's house. You wanted to leave so you can get home just to go hang out at the bar. You never think about me. You never think for one moment that maybe I wanted to spend quality time with my sister."

Your husband responds by saying, "FOR THE LOVE OF GOD, BRENDA! JUST LET IT GO. You don't see me bringing up the fact that you never cook anymore. I don't say anything about that time we were on vacation and you got so wasted that I had to cut the last night short to tend to your needs. Everything is always about you. Get over it."

We went from an issue with the toilet seat being left up, to being inconsiderate and hanging out at the bar, to Brenda not cooking and the couple having to cut their vacation short. Adding more disagreements to the mix just creates more frustration. It makes the other party become defensive and the banter can continue for hours, sometimes even weeks or more, with no resolution. Stick to one disagreement at a time. If you absolutely must add to the disagreement, you can do so in a manner that will likely make the other party not feel the need to be so defensive.

Handling One Dispute at a Time

1. Handling one dispute at a time will take lots of practice and patience, especially if you have other topics that have been really frustrating you. However, waiting to bring up your own disputes will allow you and the other party to strategically move from one issue to the next with more ease and flexibility.

2. Allow the other party to state their grievances without interruption. This will give you the opportunity to learn their point of view without providing your own point of view.

3. If you have not reached a solution, place the dispute on "pause" until you both have had a chance to think about the situation in its entirety. Often times, disputes can be revisited at a later time if needed.

Chapter 7
Be Patient

We live in a society where the majority of people have short attention spans. Often times it is hard to focus on one thing so when you continuously add multiple things to the equation, it makes you almost want to just throw in the towel and walk away, leaving resolutions hanging in the balance.

Also, keep in mind that the majority of people want instant gratification. Like really, who wants to spend time working towards something, when you can just pay money and get similar results, faster? The world of dispute resolution is a tad bit different.

Mediators and Arbitrators, like myself, understand that it can take hours, sometimes over several sessions, to reach an agreement. It is a process that takes time because so often, the issues have been building up for several years. Do you think I can effectively mediate a divorce in 30 minutes if the parties have been married for 30 years? Sure, it is possible but extremely unlikely.

While everything on social media points to fast and easy solutions, the real world is a little different.

Conflicts, problems, and issues usually build up over time, especially in long-term friendships and relationships. It is not uncommon for one party to be more passive than the other, resulting in unresolved conflicts and more often than not, built up frustrations and anger.

I used to be the passive person who allowed my anger to build up until the smallest thing would make me lose my shit. Then, I would seemingly let everything out. I would bring up things from years ago that should have been irrelevant but they obviously weren't irrelevant to me. It was quite ridiculous.

During the process of attempting to find resolutions for your conflicts, you must practice patience. Remember, a patient person has more opportunities by giving themselves time to consider all aspects of a dispute and taking a strategic look at the possible solutions. The person who is most patient usually is the one who has the most power. Yep, you read that right. The person who is the most patient usually is the one who has the most power.

Do you have thin patience? It's ok Kween, flip the page for a few tips on increasing your patience.

Tips to Help Increase Patience

1. If the other person begins to become defensive, don't join them by also becoming defensive. Use this time to take a deep breath and again, ponder on how to respond.

2. Strategically think about your next move. Take careful note of your body language while strategically thinking of your next move.

3. Give the other party a chance to calm down. Maybe drink a glass of water while the other person continues to explain their point of view but remain focused on what is being said at the same time.

Chapter 8
Now You Are a Peace Kween

So, I have given you the playbook to go from *Drama Queen to Peace Kween* by giving you *Seven Steps to Live Peacefully in Your Kweendom*™, now let's recap:

1. Clarify the disagreement
2. Figure out the common goal
3. Listen
4. Focus on the solution
5. NO personal attacks
6. Stick to one dispute at a time
7. Be patient

If you can hold onto these seven little nuggets during the dispute resolution process, you can increase your chances of resolving your disputes efficiently. And because disputes are usually a result of misunderstandings, miscommunications, frustrations, and/or personal conflicts, these seven gems will help you filter through the muck and sit pretty in your Kweendom™.

FAQs
Answers for The Peace Kween

1. Do I need an attorney for mediation?

Having an attorney is NOT a requirement for mediation. However, there are circumstances where it may be a good idea to seek legal representation.

2. What is the mediation process?

The Mediation Process:

A. Prior to Mediation, you will receive a brief questionnaire to complete.

B. On the day of Mediation, the mediator will bring both parties together in the conference room. You will be briefed on the entire process. Each party will also have the opportunity to share their position and their ideal resolution. This entire process is confidential. Nothing shared in the mediation session can be used in court.

C. Together, we will work together and begin the mediation process in good-faith, in an effort to achieve resolution.

D. If needed, all parties will have the opportunity to speak with the mediator separately in an effort to better understand each party's position. These individual sessions are also completely confidential.

E. We will continue to work the mediation process until one of several outcomes are met.

3. What is the difference between mediation and litigation?

Mediation uses a neutral third party (mediator) who does not judge the dispute but instead, the mediator facilitates the meeting, helping the parties resolve the dispute. In mediation you have control over the outcome of your case.

Litigation is often time-consuming, expensive, and unpredictable. In litigation, the judge decides the outcome of your case.

4. What is Pro Se Divorce? And how can it help someone?

Pro Se is just a fancy way of saying "self-represented". So essentially, the person did not hire an attorney but instead will represent him/herself.

Mediation can save you time and money. And the best part is, this CONFIDENTIAL service allows you to have total control over the outcome of your divorce.

If you do represent yourself but find that you need help with the paperwork, Mingo Mediation Services has several attorneys in network that you can speak with and they will help you prepare paperwork.

5. I need to work out a custody agreement. Do I have to be married to use your services?

Absolutely not. Mingo Mediation specializes in unmarried child custody cases and can facilitate your mediation with you and your child/children's other parent.

DISCLAIMER *MINGO MEDIATION SERVICES AND/OR ITS AFFILIATES DOES NOT PROVIDE LEGAL ADVICE, FINANCIAL ADVICE, MEDICAL ADVICE, OR ANY OTHER PROFESSIONAL SERVICES ADVICE.*

For more frequently asked questions, please visit: https://mingomediation.com/faq/

Acknowledgments

I humbly thank my God, husband, children, parents, grandparents, friends, mentors, and loved ones.

Special thanks to my business coach and mentor, Coach Tajuana (The LinkedIn Professor), for encouraging me to write this book.

But most importantly, I thank myself because I believed in myself even on those dark days that I did not want to get out of bed.

Point. Blank. Period.

www.ingramcontent.com/pod-product-compliance
Lightning Source LLC
Chambersburg PA
CBHW030535220526
45463CB00007B/2846